Working Dogs

Contents

Not Just Pets

Most dogs are pets,
but some go to work!
Working dogs have interesting jobs.
They help people
in many different ways.

A Dog's Nose

A dog has a much stronger
sense of smell than we do.
Many working dogs use
their noses on the job.

Dogs can learn to track down
lost people, missing pets,
money, and many other things.

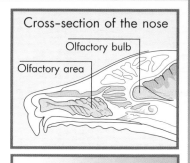

Cross-section of the nose

Olfactory bulb

Olfactory area

Dogs have about
25 times more
smell receptors
than humans do.
A dog's sense of
smell is 1,000 to
10,000 times
better than
that of humans.

These dogs are part of a police team.

Some dogs use their noses
to tell if people are sick.
One dog sniffed and sniffed at a spot
on his owner's skin.
Finally, his owner showed the spot
to her doctor.

The spot turned out to be cancer.
After the doctor removed the spot,
the owner was healthy again.
Her dog saved her life!

Helping People Feel Better

Everyone knows that dogs can't read.
But they can listen.
Children practice reading aloud
to them.

The dogs don't care if children
read slowly or make mistakes.
This helps children feel better about
reading and become better readers.

Reading dogs are trained to be good listeners.

9

Comfort dogs help
to cheer people up
and make them feel better.
Some comfort dogs live in hospitals,
and others just come for visits.

Some comfort dogs make
good companions for older people.

Service Dogs

There are people who aren't able to do certain things for themselves.

Service dogs to the rescue!

These dogs learn to open the door, turn on the light, and even pull a wheelchair.

Seeing eye dogs help people who are unable to see get around safely.

Other Unusual Jobs

Do you think these are funny jobs
for dogs to have? There are many more.

Hearing dogs	let hearing-impaired owner know when a baby cries, or when a doorbell rings
Lifeguard dogs	rescue people from the water
Bowling alley dogs	fetch fallen pins the machine can't reach
Herd dogs	guard and herd sheep

No matter how hard a dog works,
he doesn't get a paycheck.
He works for food,
good care, and love.

Index